Animal Tales For Today

Volume 1

by Michael Heal

Illustrations by James Cottell

GW01044228

First Published in 2023.
All rights reserved.
Text Michael Heal © 2022.
Illustrations James Cottell © 2022
ISBN: 978-1-915787-29-3

No portion of this book may be reproduced in any form or by any means
(which includes mechanically, electronically, or by any other means, including
photocopying), without written permission from the author.
Permission should be addressed in writing to:
michaelhealpr@gmail.com

For My Daughter Zara

Abigail, the ant, has her role in the nest.
She works all day long without taking a rest.
Fetching and carrying food for the queen,
And standing on guard when intruders are seen.

She lives with her family under the ground,
In dim, dusty corridors which muffle the sound
Of adults and children walking above,
On lawns and on patios, which they all love.

"Now, don't bite the children", young Abby is told,
"Because, if you do, you won't be so bold
When hot water and chemicals they pour on our home,
To drive us away and again we must roam".

Belinda, the butterfly, is a marvellous sight.
With bright coloured wings, she is graceful in flight.
Taking her time to visit the plants,
She does all she can to help nature advance.

She must lay down her eggs in a place safe from storms,
And hope that the sun will still keep them warm.
As new lives develop, they are fragile and small,
And need time to grow in their light, flimsy ball.

Caterpillars emerge and eat eggshells and leaves,
Shedding their skins as quick as you please.
Then the chrysalis forms and, inside that tight sack,
A butterfly takes shape, with both wings intact.

A new life breaks out and, before very long,
Its wings have dried out – efficient and strong.

Belinda won't see what she's achieved,
Her lifespan is short, so young children please,
Make sure, when you see, a fine butterfly,
You rejoice in its beauty, for soon it may die.

Chloe, the cat, is a graceful Siamese.
Alone in the garden she did as she pleased.
Grooming her coat is the first task of the day,
To show off her beauty to neighbours and strays.

The sparrows in the garden are tempting to chase,
But soon have her running all over the place.
The birds seem to sense when she is near,
Pecking at crumbs, displaying no fear.

But, when Chloe pounces, she catches nothing but air,
And she finds it hard to believe just why they aren't there.
The reason for this, well, it's easy to tell,
Around Chloe's neck hangs a bright, tinkling bell.

Daniel, the dolphin, was swimming along,
Out in the wide ocean, where the waves were quite strong.
When, all of a sudden, Dan dives out of sight,
Drawn down to the depths by a powerful light.

What could it be, flashing bright from below?
Gold, diamonds, emeralds, does anyone know?
Daniel goes closer, so keen to explore
A scene he's never encountered before.

But when he arrives at the source of the light,
The image he sees simply gives him a fright.
A rotting old shipwreck lies on the seabed,
With rows of white skeletons each nodding his head.

Eric, the elephant, is in a very strange mood.
His trunk drags the floor and he is right off his food.
His friends try to bribe him with cakes and a bun,
But nothing can tempt him to join in their fun.

"What's the matter, young man?" his uncle asks with concern,
"You're acting so miserable, have you taken a turn?
Is it your tummy, your back or your head?
If you don't improve soon, you'd better take to your bed".

Eric's body feels different, he is growing you see,
Like all children do, quite naturally.
Then it all becomes clear, when just after dusk,
Young Eric is sprouting his very first tusk.

Jasmine, the jaguar, is a powerful cat,
The most accomplished of hunters, she's famous for that.
On land or in water, she hunts without fear,
For turtles or fish, monkeys, rodents and deer.

Lightning fast on the ground and a powerful swimmer,
This fierce, clever cat rarely lacks for a dinner.
Her home is the rain forest, now under attack,
By human encroachment, now it's time to turn back.

They're chopping down trees as fast as they can,
With never a thought for nature's grand plan.
Let's pray for Jasmine and her growing young brood,
For it's much harder now to find them their food.

Kylie, the kangaroo, was in a terrible state.
Her son Joey was missing and it was getting quite late.
Safe in her pouch, he had continued to grow,
But now there were places he wanted to go.

She knew he sought freedom, the urge to explore,
But how would he cope with this desire to see more?
The wide open grasslands and mountains so high,
The rivers and forests that stretch to the sky.

Then Kylie heard screaming, a voice she knew well.
Of course it was Joey, it was easy to tell.

Kylie followed the cries and arrived there to see,
A frightened young Joey looking up at a tree.
"It's a monster with big eyes, out on the prowl"
"Don't be silly", laughed Kylie, "It's only Oscar the owl".

Lisa, the ladybird, hovers around,
Looking for plants that stand tall in the ground.
Circling the garden, she chooses with care,
For the lives of her children depend on that stare.

She selects a green leaf and lands from above,
Lays her eggs in a cluster, with pride and with love.
Her bright red markings mean danger, stay away,
Designed to keep enemies and predators at bay.

But she's a friend to us all, and so are her kids,
They protect all the plants by eating aphids.
Leave her alone and allow her some space,
And flowers will prosper in their natural place.

Rejoice in her presence and, as she takes to the air,
Pray her eggs produce babies, even though she's not there.

Micky, the monkey, moves through the trees.
With long arms and a tail, he does it with ease.
Not for him an existence confined to the ground,
He much prefers life just swinging around.

He lives with his family, a sociable bunch,
And there's always a relative who comes to share lunch.
They look after each other with grooming each day,
But always make time for laughter and play.

Micky lives on the food that the forest provides,
Eating leaves and fresh fruit, that's how he survives.
But there's one that's a favourite, the one he likes best,
It's a lovely banana, it beats all the rest.

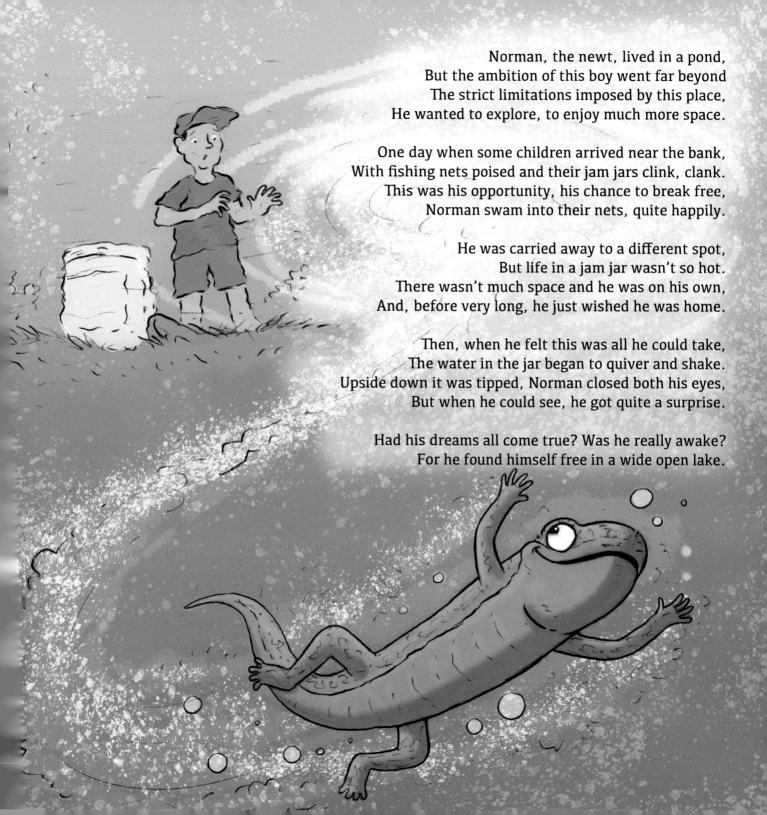

Norman, the newt, lived in a pond,
But the ambition of this boy went far beyond
The strict limitations imposed by this place,
He wanted to explore, to enjoy much more space.

One day when some children arrived near the bank,
With fishing nets poised and their jam jars clink, clank.
This was his opportunity, his chance to break free,
Norman swam into their nets, quite happily.

He was carried away to a different spot,
But life in a jam jar wasn't so hot.
There wasn't much space and he was on his own,
And, before very long, he just wished he was home.

Then, when he felt this was all he could take,
The water in the jar began to quiver and shake.
Upside down it was tipped, Norman closed both his eyes,
But when he could see, he got quite a surprise.

Had his dreams all come true? Was he really awake?
For he found himself free in a wide open lake.

Oscar, the owl, was a bird everyone knew.
He was old, he was wise and he had quite a few
Grey feathers, which gave some hint of his age,
But mention of this only prompted his rage.

Although older than most, he was sprightly and fit,
Still a match for the young ones and able to pit
His wits against their fizz and their pop,
And in all sorts of contests, he came out on top.

The more mature birds saw him as a friend,
And enjoyed the advice he was willing to lend
On all kinds of subjects from science to art,
Glad of the knowledge his words could impart.

But, there is much more to Oscar than learning and sums.
Owls love the night life and want to have fun.
So, next time at the disco, when the lights go down low,
Those bright eyes in the corner, they could be Oscar's you know.

Patricia, the pig, found it hard to make friends.
She was quick to insult but slow to commend.
She felt she was superior to all of the rest,
And, on every occasion, she always knew best.

She felt nothing of eating more than her share,
And was first at the trough when the food landed there.
She bullied the young ones who trembled in fear
At the sound of her voice and when she was near.

Something was needed to bring about change,
Which only the farmer could hope to arrange.
They all held their breath to see what was in store,
Then cheered as she was led to the pigsty next door.

Quentin, the quail, had a terrible fright,
For the sound of loud gun shots, though still out of sight,
Meant the hunters were coming and looking for sport,
To eat at their table with wine and with port.

Close by, was a thicket which gave him a chance
To disappear from view without attracting a glance.
He would hide in the branches without making a sound,
And wait for the humans to pass by on the ground.

The hunters shouted to scare out their prey,
But Quentin was motionless, quite still he must stay,
'Til the gunfire and barking had all come to rest,
To give him the chance to fly home, safe to his nest.

Xavier, the small X-Ray fish, is not often seen.
In South America he lives, in rivers and streams.
He is not very big and looks easy prey,
For much larger predators, if he swims in their way.

But, Xavier is clever, his hearing so clear,
He can avoid danger before it gets near.
And if they get close, they'll get a surprise,
For Xavier disappears, right in front of their eyes.
His body is translucent, and all they can make out,
Is the plant life behind him, that is waving about.

Yuri, the yak, lives in Tibet,
And, when the snows come, it's easy to forget
The warmth and the colour of those summer days,
Chewing lush grass in the bright morning haze.

The winters are harsh and the nights oh, so long!
And Yuri is glad when, at last, they are gone.
His long, shaggy coat helps him keep out the cold,
But he wonders just what the future will hold.

Will he be, for eternity, pulling the plough?
Or transporting farm produce, just like he does now?
What would it be like to live close to the sea?
To bathe in the ocean, to feel really free?

The others only laugh when he tells them his dreams.
"Just remember your place, life is just what it seems.
You can't change the world, you are only a yak,
We were born to work hard with weight on our back."

But Yuri can dream, he just won't give in,
For who knows just what tomorrow may bring?

Zara, the zebra, liked to have fun,
And, at all kinds of parties, she was the one
Who started the dancing and encouraged the rest
To enjoy the occasion and make it the best.

Zara always had rhythm and was light on her feet,
And it didn't take long for her to pick up the beat.
No matter the music, right from the start,
She spurred on the others to take a full part.

When you watch zebras dancing, you might get a surprise,
For the stripes on their bodies play tricks with your eyes.
It's really quite hard to tell which zebra is which,
Like a shimmering heat haze, a conjuring trick.

It's just what they all do when they sense danger is near,
To confuse all their predators, they simply huddle in fear.
So, when lions and cheetahs try to pick out a kill,
Their eyes cannot focus, the herd just won't keep still.

Their vision confused, the big cats slink away,
Leaving Zara and the herd safe for today.

About the author and illustrator

Michael first created Animal Tales For Today as bedtime stories for his young daughter, Zara, when she was at primary school and she has always encouraged him to share them with a much wider audience.

After teaching both History and English in the Caribbean and the U.K., Michael went into sports journalism and then set up his own sports events and marketing company. He lives with his wife Pamela in West Sussex.

James studied illustration at University College Falmouth and has been a professional illustrator for over 15 years. His clients include Buster Books, Oxford University Press, HarperCollins, Franklin Watts, Atebol and Award Publications.

He lives in Devon and is rarely without his trusty sketchbook to capture the world around him. His favourite things to draw are dogs, dinosaurs and trees.

Follow him on Instagram and Twitter @jamescottell.

Coming Soon - Animal Tales For Today Volume 2